BECOME
A PEOPLE
MAGNET

Marc Reklau is a coach, speaker and a bestselling author. Marc's mission is to empower people to create the life they want and to give them the resources and tools to make it happen.

His message is simple: Many people want to change things in their lives, but few are willing to do a simple set of exercises constantly over a period of time. You can plan and create success and happiness in your life by installing habits that support you on the way to your goals.

If you want to work with Marc directly, contact him on his homepage www.marcreklau.com, where you also find more information about him.

You can connect with him on Twitter @MarcReklau, Facebook or on his website www.goodhabitsacademy.com.

HOW TO BECOME A PEOPLE MAGNET

62 LIFE-CHANGING TIPS
TO ATTRACT EVERYONE YOU MEET

MARC REKLAU

RUPA

Published by
Rupa Publications India Pvt. Ltd 2019
7/16, Ansari Road, Daryaganj
New Delhi 110002

Sales centres:
Allahabad Bengaluru Chennai
Hyderabad Jaipur Kathmandu
Kolkata Mumbai

Copyright © Marc Reklau 2019
English language edition for Indian Subcontinent only arranged through
Montse Cortazar Literary Agency (www.montsecortazar.com).

The views and opinions expressed in this book are the author's
own and the facts are as reported by him/her which have been
verified to the extent possible, and the publishers are not in any
way liable for the same.

ISBN: 978-93-5333-473-4

Eighteenth impression 2022

25 24 23 22 21 20 19 18

Printed in India

Disclaimer

CONTENTS

Part III: Basic Rules

Part IV: Lead by Example

Part V: If You Have to Say it, Say it Smoothly

INTRODUCTION

Your success and happiness in life, to a great extent, depends on how you get along with other people. Are you able to influence and persuade them? Although success can mean something entirely different for each person, there is one common denominator—other people.

Les Giblin mentions in his book *The Art of Dealing with People* that 'various scientific studies have proven that if you learn to deal with other people, you will have gone 85 per cent of the way down the road to success in any business, occupation, or profession, and about 99 per cent of the way to happiness.' I agree completely. Although, I teach that everyone is 100 per cent responsible for their own happiness, people are a huge factor and can influence your happiness or unhappiness enormously.

I have good news for you. Good guys DO NOT finish last anymore. If you get along well with people, doors will open where there were none before. We have to learn to get along with people so that we can be happy and at the same time leave our counterpart's ego intact.

The most successful people are usually the ones who best get along with people—of course; there are always exceptions to the rule. Science tells us that the #1 predictor of success and lasting happiness is our social relationships. People with a strong social network even live longer!

The most successful people, quite often, aren't the ones with superior intelligence or the best skills, and the happiest people most times aren't smarter than we are, yet they are the ones who have the greatest people skills.

You cannot force people to like you—and this book is not about people-pleasing—but if you work on your people skills, you will see that people in some magical way co-operate more willingly with you, appreciate you more, and finally give you the approval and acceptance you've always craved for—and the best is that it will all happen naturally. Remember 'What goes around comes around.' If you now think, 'I will work on my people skills when people start accepting me more,' that's like being thirsty and saying, 'I will drink when I'm not thirsty anymore.' Don't wait. Start practicing your people skills now.

In this book, you will learn specific principles that you can start practicing right away. Most of them are common sense, but it's always good to have a reminder, because as they say 'Common sense is the least common of all senses.'

The times are over when you could force people to act as you want, or force them to give you what you want. The best strategy as of today is to learn the skills of dealing with people.

Let's get to work!

Part I

....

First Things First

1

UNDERSTANDING
HUMAN NATURE

If you want to develop people skills, the first thing you have to do is obvious—You have to understand people. You have to know why we do the things we do and how we react in certain circumstances. Understanding people means recognizing them for what they are—not for what you want them to be, nor for what you think they are, but for what they really are.

So, what are they? Let's get the elephant out of the room right in the beginning.

People are, above all, interested in themselves. Yup. Sorry. No matter who you are, people will always be a thousand times more interested in themselves than in you. No judgment here.

I bet that you are also a thousand times more interested in yourself than in other people, right?

No worries. That's ok. It's human nature. Really, no judgment here. Just accept this uncomfortable truth. You can be a thousand times more interested in yourself than in other people, and still do good things for them—but we will get to that later.

People's actions are governed by self-interest. Period. As

I said before, that in itself is not a bad thing. You don't have to become all apologetic or embarrassed. It's human nature. It has always been this way and it probably always will be. It's something we all have in common.

In every human relationship, your counterpart will always think or ask themselves, 'what's in it for me?' Remember this question, 'What's in it for me?' By the way, you're asking this question in all your interactions too, consciously or subconsciously.

Does this all sound too negative? Well, it gets better right now. Once you have accepted this truth, you can use it successfully in all your interactions with people. You will see in the following chapters that many successful techniques of dealing with and influencing people stem from this understanding.

People are above all interested in themselves and not in you.

2

THE MOST IMPORTANT SUBJECT OF
ANY CONVERSATION

Are you ready to polish your conversation skills? Do you want to know the most important and ultimately the most interesting subject in the world that any person would love to talk about with you?

Ready? Okay. Here it is:

The most important subject that anyone will want to talk about with you is... THEMSELVES.

I'm sorry if I sound cynical, but it is what it is. Stay with me, though. This book will change your relationships and interactions with others. Just stay with me.

So, when you talk with people about themselves, they will love you for your wise choice of subject. They will be totally fascinated by the subject and show an enormous interest. Have you ever been to a networking meeting or a social event and had to talk to a person who was just talking about themselves all the time? How did it feel? Were you very attracted to that person? Did you want to spend more time with them? Or were you just waiting for a reason to get the hell out of Dodge City?

On the other hand, you might have talked to a person

with people skills who talked about you the entire time, who asked questions, and was interested in you, wanting to know what and how you are doing? How did that feel?

Who of those two persons would you prefer to be around?

When you are talking to people, forget about 'I', 'my', and 'mine' for a while and substitute it with a word that will make you a very sought after conversational partner: The word 'YOU'.

'What can I do for YOU?' 'Is there anything I can help YOU with?' 'This can be very beneficial for YOU.' 'How are YOU today?' 'What are YOUR favourite...?'

When you get from 'I', 'my', 'mine', to 'YOU' and 'YOUR' your power and influence will increase by a significant degree.

Do you want to know another way of using people's interest in themselves? Here it comes: get them talking about themselves. Who doesn't love to talk about themselves? If you can show true interest and get people to talk about themselves, they will like you a lot, so ask them lots of questions about themselves.

'How is everything going Barney? How is your family doing? How are things at_____? What have you been up to since our last meeting?'

Stop talking about yourself and start talking about the person in front of you or get them to talk about themselves.

3

MAKE PEOPLE FEEL IMPORTANT

What makes people tick? What makes people do the things they do, good and bad?

The desire to be recognized. The desire to be important. The desire to be noticed. The desire to be 'someone.' This is the most powerful motivator. It's the reason for doing good things and unfortunately, for a twisted mind, also the reason for doing bad things.

We can use this universal trait of humanity to take our human relationships to the next level. I can't mention it often enough, of course, your interest in the other person must be real. We want to use these techniques to become people magnets and influencers, not to manipulate people.

Whenever people talk about the greatest people magnets and most skilful leaders, they say something like: 'He made everybody feel special,' 'She made everybody feel like they were the most important person in the room.'

This is where we want to get. This is what we want people to say about us one day. Make people feel important. The more important you make them feel, the better they will respond. Yes, you have this power. You can make any person like themselves better. Make them feel appreciated.

Give every person you meet the importance they deserve, which is almost definitely the importance YOU think YOU deserve. Don't ignore them, don't talk down on them. Make them feel important. Listen to them! If you don't listen, they feel unimportant. Compliment them, but only if it's a sincere compliment.

Recognition and appreciation are so important. They make us function better under any circumstance. Use their name as often as you can. People like to be called by their names. Let them finish their sentence. Don't interrupt people. Make a short pause before answering. This gives them the feeling that you have listened closely and are interested in what they have to say. You can also nod while they are talking to show that you are following. Remember chapter 2. Use 'You' and 'Your.' Avoid 'I, mine, my, me.' If you are in a group, don't ignore people. Pay attention to everyone.

So, to make other people feel important first of all YOU have to think they ARE important. Secondly, you have to notice them. When you notice people you are showing them, 'You are important to me.' And thirdly don't forget that you are no different as you also want to feel important.

Make people feel important, and they'll always be on your side.

4

THE MOST IMPORTANT CHARACTERISTIC: AGREE WITH PEOPLE

This technique will get you very far, believe me. Nothing will help you more than being agreeable.

Why?

Well, first of all, people like people who agree with them. Second, people don't like people who disagree with them. Third, people don't like being disagreed with. Am I right or am I right?

Adopt the attitude of being agreeable. Learn to agree with people and let them know when you do so. Nod your head. Say 'yes,' 'right,' 'I totally agree with you,' 'I totally get you.'

As they say, 'Any fool can disagree with people' (and most fools probably do). Agreeing with people, on the other hand, is a wise, intelligent and good decision, even more so when the other person is wrong. Only disagree with people if you have absolutely no other choice. No worries. It will happen less often than you think. When you are about to disagree with someone, always have in mind the magic question, 'Do I want to be right or do I want to be in peace?'

In no case argue! I repeat: Don't argue—even if you are

right. Why? Easy: Nobody ever wins an argument. Both lose. One loses, and the other one loses even if he or she is right. You also don't win a lot of friends by arguing, do you? Who wants to be friends with a person that argues all the time anyway?

So don't argue, and don't even think of fighting! Refuse to fight! Some people might even want to provoke you because they love fighting. They feed on fights. There's a saying in Spain: 'If one doesn't want to fight, two won't fight.' Ignore the fighters. Change the subject, walk away. Whatever—You don't want fighters as friends anyway.

If you make a mistake, admit it. It's a sign of a strong person, and you'll be admired for it, as average and mediocre people don't admit their mistakes. They will rather lie, deny or find excuses.

Remember, people like people who agree with them.

5

HOW TO MAKE PEOPLE
LIKE YOU IMMEDIATELY

'You never get a second chance to make a first impression.' Old? Yes! Cheesy? Maybe! But also true as the truth gets. Experts say that people subconsciously decide if they like us or not in a couple of seconds. The first few seconds decide in which direction a relationship will go. Once this decision is made, it is very, very difficult to change it. The person you have just met already knows if he or she wants to go out with you. The HR executive already knows if he or she will offer you a job or not when you stick your nose through the door. They might not be aware of it yet, but they know.

Do you know how you can make most people friendly, cooperative and polite in those first few seconds?

SMILE—and smile a lot!

In the first moment when the door opens, when you make eye contact, even before you say anything; give the person your most sincere smile. A smile can do miracles. Did you ever try it?

Smile at the baker, the butcher, in the subway, at the newspaper stand and see what happens.

Smile even when you are talking on the phone! The person

on the other end of the phone will notice it.

Smiling is contagious, so in most cases, people will smile back and be nice to you. Mostly in human relationships, you will get right back what you put out to other people. What goes around comes around. Be nice to people and people will be nice to you. Be rude, and people will be rude. Of course, there are always exceptions to the rule. So, if you are nice and your counterpart is rude...become even nicer! The meaner they get, the nicer you get. Make it a challenge. Nobody can resist long against sincere politeness, a good heart, and a smile.

By the way...smiling is not only good for your relationships, but also for your health! Science has demonstrated that laughing or smiling a lot daily improves your mental state and creativity. It also alters your stress response in difficult situations by slowing down your heart rate and decreasing stress levels. Smiling sends a signal to your brain that things are all right. One study has even found a link between smiling and longevity! Smiling people are perceived as more confident and more likely to be trusted. People just feel good around them.

Smile and win in all relationships.

6

HOW TO MAKE A GOOD IMPRESSION

You teach people how to treat you by the way you treat yourself. If you want to make a good impression, giving yourself the value you deserve is crucial. Before expecting people to value you, think well of you, and admire you, YOU have to value you, think well of you and admire you. Do you follow?

You can't expect others to believe in you if you don't believe in you, yet. Start being proud of yourself, of who you are, of where you come from, and of what you do for a living. This is not the time to be modest! Careful though. It's also not the time to be arrogant. I'm talking about healthy self-esteem. Knowing who you are, knowing your strength, but also knowing that you are not better than anybody else (and remembering that nobody is better than you either).

You can influence the opinion of other people about you through your behaviour. Behave in a way that will have a positive effect on people.

Handle yourself with pride and confidence. Be sincere with people. Say only things you mean and mean the things you say. As I mentioned before, cheap compliments, empty promises, and meaningless words will always be discovered and cause the opposite effect of what you want to achieve. Always keep in mind that it takes months and years to build a good reputation, but only seconds to destroy it. If you show genuine passion and enthusiasm, it will be difficult to resist you and to not like you. Enthusiasm is contagious.

There are also some 'don'ts' that can hinder making a good impression, like being overanxious. Being overanxious makes people wonder, and they start doubting. 'Why is he so anxious?', 'What does she have to hide?'

Never try to make yourself look good, by putting other people down. This makes you look bad and can damage your effort to make friends and influence people. Remember—a person that treats you nicely and disrespects the waiter is not a nice person. Stay away from people like that and most importantly: Don't be like that (or people will stay away from you).

Make the following your golden rule: If you can't say nice things, say nothing. Don't put people down.

Other people's opinion about us is primarily made by how we behave.

7

HOW TO CONNECT WITH PEOPLE

One great way to connect with people is by being interested in them and in the things that interest them.

In Barcelona, and probably in many other places, usually, you make friends easily by talking about the city's seemingly most important subject: Football. It doesn't even matter how the local team is doing; there's always something to talk about.

Find out what interests people and then start a conversation about it. This can help you in making new friends as well as in business relationships and opportunities too.

Today it's easier than ever. If you go to a business meeting, conference or networking event you can find out people's interests on social media. If you make an effort to study their interests, you'll surely get good results. I know a lot of salesperson who know everything that can interest their client even before they have met them the first time in person. Those are also the most successful salesperson. They talk about the interests of their potential clients with true interest and then close the sale.

Become genuinely interested in other people and talk in terms of other people's interests!

If you want to really connect with people, you need to

show some real interest in them. You have to get away from the 'I,' 'I,' 'I,' the trying to impress people with your achievements and go towards becoming genuinely interested in other people.

Attraction starts with little things like being friendly, just greeting people (you won't believe how many people are so self-absorbed, they don't even greet people). Be nice. Even on the phone. If you are smiling on the phone, the person on the other end of the line can feel it.

Have in mind that people like to be admired, remember their birthdays, do things for people. When people notice that you are interested in them, they will become interested in you. But your interest must be sincere. People can smell false praise and played interest from a mile away.

Show true interest in other people and succeed.

8

HOW TO DEVELOP
AN ATTRACTIVE PERSONALITY

Going through life, we all want to be liked. We want to have friends. We want to be interesting. We want to feel important. We want to attract friends and clients naturally. I'm sure you know people who are like that. So, how are they doing it? And even more importantly... how can YOU develop these abilities?

One of the most important ingredients is, Acceptance. You must accept people as they are. So simple and yet sometimes so complicated, right? To make it easier remember these things. People are not like you. They are not perfect (you also aren't, and—even better—you don't have to be!). You can't change them no matter how hard you try. They might not have the same values as you and many times they won't live up to your high expectations.

So, I'll make it easy for you: Accept and like people just as they are. On the long run, that will be more influential than any advice or lectures, you have to give.

Another ingredient is Approval. No matter how many faults somebody has, you can always find something to approve of. Let people know it because seeing these things and mentioning them will make them grow. Remember our hunger for acknowledgment? If you start approving of character traits in people, you will satisfy this hunger, and you will probably make these people work on their other character traits and skills to gain more approval. Praise people and watch them grow.

Last but not least the third ingredient, Appreciation. Next to love, appreciation is probably the most critical force in the universe. Why do our marriages and jobs go sour? When we don't appreciate them anymore. When we don't appreciate what we have. And how do we make happiness and success grow? Appreciating what we have. Appreciate your spouse, your children, your employees, your boss, your clients and the most important thing—let them know that you appreciate them. Be grateful. An excellent way to show your appreciation is to tell them, but there is more you can do. Don't keep people waiting. Be punctual. Let them know you will be with them as soon as possible. Thank people. A very powerful way is to write people a thank you note or letter. Treat people as special. Remember that we all want to be recognized for our uniqueness and worth.

Accept. Approve of. Appreciate. Use this formula to become a people magnet.

9

IT'S WHAT THEY WANT,
NOT WHAT YOU WANT

When you want to influence people always have in mind: It's what they want, not what you want.

I love the example Dale Carnegie put in his classic, *How to Make Friends and Influence People*.

He loved strawberry and cream, but when he went fishing he didn't use strawberries with cream to bait the fish, but worms. Fish want worms, not strawberries.

In human life, it's the same. We are interested in what we want but nobody else is. Everybody else is just like us. They are interested in what they want.

So if we want to influence others, we have to talk about what they want and show them how to get it.

We have to put ourselves in their shoes and see things from their point of view.

We have to make them really, really want what we have to offer them. We have to speak their language, use the words they would use and talk in terms of what they want.

If you can show them how you can help them and focus on what they want instead of what you want. If you can show them how you can solve their problems, then my friend, you have more new clients, partners, or friends.

As a salesman, for example, you have to think what your client needs. Which problem can you solve for them? Which advantages does your product have? Where and how are you better than your competitors? As a leader or spouse, you have to put yourself in their shoes? What do your employees or your spouse need from you? Motivation? Acknowledgement? Praise? Gratitude? Those usually never fail.

The more you think about the needs and want of other people, the more successful relationships you will get. Be careful though and don't forget your own needs and wants.

Remember: It's what they want, not what you want.

Part II

Communicate Effectively

10

LISTEN TO PEOPLE ACTIVELY

One of the most critical skills of a 'people magnet' is the ability and skill of 'active listening' or listening profoundly. The more you listen, the smarter you will get. You will also be more liked, and people will love to have conversations with you. Why? Because you'll be of a rare breed. Most people never listen.

A good listener will always have the advantage over a good talker because he or she always allows people to hear their favourite speaker in the world: themselves.

While too much talking gives you away, listening will make you look a lot smarter, because you're giving importance to what the other person has to say instead of bragging with your knowledge.

So, how do you become a good listener? Here we go:

Listening profoundly means to listen to the person in front of you while giving them your full attention. Look at the person who is talking. Listen with your eyes, with your ears, with your whole body and keep looking at them. Nod your head to show them you are agreeing with their points and smile.

Lean towards the speaker. Show interest. Show them you don't want to miss a single word. Ask questions. This will show the speaker that you are listening and will flatter him/her. It can be super simple questions like, 'and then what happened' or 'and then what did you do?'

Quiet down the little voice in your head that comes up with advice or a solution, thirty seconds after the speaker starts speaking. Don't listen to answer. Listen to understand. If you are rehearsing what you are going to say next, you are not listening! Don't interrupt the speaker until he or she is finished, or don't just wait for your counterpart to pause so that you can begin to speak. Don't change subjects. On the contrary ask for more.

If you want to give advice, ask for permission. Most of the time the person who is speaking will come up with the solution—if you let her or him finish.

Don't forget using 'you' and 'your' instead of 'me, my, mine.'

Try it! Becoming a good listener will take your conversations and relationships to an entirely new level. When people feel that you are listening to them, they will automatically like to be around you.

Be a good listener!

11

BECOME AN INFLUENCER

Influencing people means to get them to do what you want them to do. So, the logical first step will be to find out what will make them do it. You need to know what they want. You need to know what will motivate them, what will move them. The biggest mistake we make when trying to influence people is that we think that other people like what we like, are motivated by things that motivate us, are after what we are after. Well. In most cases, they are not. Everybody is different. Everyone has different values. Everyone likes different things, and everyone has different motivators.

To influence people, you need to find out what they want. Once you know what they want, you can make them take action by telling them what they want to hear.

You show them how they can get what they want by doing what you want them to do. Yup. That's manipulating at its best—so I hope dear reader that you just wish the best for the people you want to influence because this power—just like the power of electricity or the atom—can be used to create something beautiful or to destroy. Choose wisely.

First of all, you will have to find out what people want, what they are looking for. If they want security, talk security.

If they want to leave their day job, show them ways to leave their day job, if they want financial freedom, you talk financial freedom. The point is to find out what people want and then, show them how to get what they want by doing what you want them to do (e.g., buy the course, buy the clothes, come to work for you, etc.).

If you are looking for a job, you would first find out what the employer is looking for, what abilities and responsibilities are needed for the job, and then you would show them that you can fill these needs better than anybody else.

When you know what somebody is looking for, you can talk the language they want to hear.

So, from now on listen very carefully to what people say, watch with great interest what they do and ask lots of questions. Make an effort to find out what people want and then use it to influence them.

Find out what people want most.

12

HOW TO CONVINCE PEOPLE REAL QUICK

Most of the time people you meet will be skeptical of you and of what you say. No worries. That's human. Whatever you are saying they will think that you probably want to sell them something (a product, your best version and so on) and people don't like to be sold to. They like to make their own decisions—or at least, feel like that they are making their own decisions.

A great way to convince people is quoting someone. That's why testimonials and opinions of others, in other words, social proof go a long, long way. Let somebody else speak for you even if the person is not present in the moment.

- If you are selling something and you are asked about the product, quote a relevant customer opinion. In that case, your customer is answering the question although he or she isn't there with you.
- If somebody wants to know if you are paying your suppliers on time, you can mention how happy your other suppliers are with you paying their bills on time.

- If you are applying for a job, mention all the good things your past employers and colleagues say about you.

Notice something? You haven't answered any one of these questions. Your customers, suppliers, former employers and colleagues have done the answering for you.

It's a psychological mystery. If you tell people directly about how great you are, they will be hugely skeptical, yet they don't have any doubts that what you tell them is true, if you tell them through a third person's testimonial.

Speak through third persons. Quote statistics and/or people. Relate facts. Tell success stories.

13

GET PEOPLE TO SAY
YES TO YOU

You probably know this already. If not, this will be a major chapter for you and can change your whole life: Getting people to say 'yes' has a lot less to do with luck or their mood than what you think.

Enjoy learning a great skill in this chapter. The ability that will boost the chances of getting people to say 'yes' to you, and don't forget: If you get them to say yes to you, you'll get them to do whatever you want them to do.

1. Give people reasons to say yes to you.
   Everyone has a reason for doing what they do. If you want somebody to do something for you, give them a reason to do it. Of course, the reason has to be to their advantage or benefit—if not they won't do it. Tell them how they will benefit by doing what you want them to do.

2. Ask 'yes' questions.
   It's easier to get a 'yes' from people if they are already in a 'yes' mindset. This is done by asking them two or more 'yes questions.' 'Yes questions' are questions that can only be answered by yes. The idea behind this technique is that

once you get people to answer three or four questions with 'Yes', it's a lot more probable that they will continue saying yes.

Do you want to be happy?

Do you want to be independent?

Do you want to live a life free from worries?

Emphasize the yes questions by nodding your head while asking the questions.

You want a great future, right? (Nodding your head)

You want the very best product, right? (Nodding your head)

3. Give them a choice between two yeses.

Don't give people a choice between yes and no. Let them choose between saying yes to one thing or yes to another thing you are offering them. Let people choose between acting the way you want them to do, one way or another. Whatever they choose, they'll say yes to you. If you want a date with Lucie, ask her:

'Would you like to meet up tomorrow afternoon or in the evening?' (I wish I were that skilled twenty-five years ago... unfortunately, then, I mostly asked yes or no questions like, 'Do you want to go on a date with me?' and mostly got a no...)

When you are giving the other party a choice between yes and no, you might hear an awful lot of nos. It's much better to not ask open questions.

'Do you want the red or the black?' instead of 'Do you want one of these?'

'Do you want to start today or on Wednesday?' instead of 'Do you want to start here?'

'Do you want to pay by cash or credit card?' instead of 'Do you want this?'

I'm not saying that this will work every single time, but your success rate will increase. It will surely work a lot better than giving people a choice between answering yes or no.

4. Expect People to Say Yes to You.

This is also called confidence. If you look back on your life, I bet that whenever you were really confident, when you really, really expected a yes—without the slightest doubt— you got a yes. So, be confident and let people know that you expect them to say yes. Of course, this technique will not work all the time, and you'll have to practice it like you practice playing tennis or golf, and then you'll get better at it.

Get the easy yes, yes and yes and more yeses will come.

14

TALK LESS, DO MORE

You are what you do, not what you say you'll do. If you want to change the world stop talking about it and start taking action. Pick up a pen and write an article or a book. Stop complaining about politicians, join a political party and become more active in politics.

Actions speak louder than words. If you want to impress and attract people don't just talk about what you are going to do for them. Show them. People who just talk about the great things they will do for their friends, their company, their community and never follow up with action lose credibility, and sooner or later, nobody is going to take them seriously anymore. What's even worse is that one day they won't even believe themselves anymore and their self-esteem will take a hit because every time we say something and don't do it, our self-esteem suffers. If we don't follow up with actions, we are mainly telling our subconscious: 'What I say doesn't matter.' And if we do it too often, we conclude, 'I don't matter, I'm worthless.' So, be careful about what you say and follow up with it.

Talk less and convince the people around you by your actions. Don't tell your friends how you are going to help them.

Help them. Don't brag about how generous you are, donate to charity. Don't tell your boss what a great worker you are, let your work and your numbers speak for themselves. (Some bosses can't see your great job, so you also have to brag about it, but that's the exception to the rule).

Stop talking and start doing. NOW.

15

RESPECT OTHER PEOPLE'S OPINIONS

Let's get one thing straight at the beginning. You won't be right all the time. And even the times when you are right, it's a lot more beneficial for you not to prove others wrong. We don't like to be proven wrong. And if we are proven wrong in a way that hurts our intelligence, our self-respect, and our pride—we surely won't admit it. It's impossible to alter people's opinions after having hurt their feelings. Saying things like, 'I'm going to prove this to you' is like saying, 'I'm smarter than you and I'm going to prove it,' and the only thing it will cause is opposition and will make it impossible to change your counterpart's opinion. If you want to prove someone wrong you have to act smarter. You can't let them know. Do it subtly so that nobody even notices that you are doing it.

Start by admitting that you could be wrong. It changes the whole conversation. You are admitting a mistake. 'I might be wrong, but let's look at it.' This doesn't cause opposition. Nobody will ever object to you saying, 'I might be wrong, but let's look at it.' instead it will stop all arguments and inspire your counterpart to be just as honest and open-minded as you.

Show respect for the other person's opinion. Put yourself in their shoes and try to understand them. Be diplomatic and courteous. You will get much further with this tactic than with just bluntly telling a person that they are wrong.

Did you ever notice that when you admit that you are wrong instead of defending yourself the other person becomes empathetic and instead of making fun of you, actually, comforts you?

If you want to be right and have to point out other people's mistakes all the time, soon, you will be alone, and nobody will want to be around you.

Use diplomacy, be smart, be subtle. Don't prove other people wrong.

16

BE AUTHENTIC.
BE TRANSPARENT. BE YOU!

If you want to be successful with people you have to be real. Be authentic. Be YOU!

Don't play any roles. Let people feel that what they see is what they get. It might be difficult at first because we're all afraid that people might not like us the way we are, but that's just another mind movie. Another creation of our mind—the world's greatest producer of soap operas and drama. Know your strengths, know your weaknesses, embrace vulnerability and take responsibility for your mistakes. That's all you have to do. Not more. Not less. People will connect with you on a deeper level! You don't have to fear the judgment of others. They will love you for being real.

The worst thing you can do is say things or agree with people just to please them. That's not being skilled with people. That's a sign of low self-esteem. Say what you really think. Of course, that doesn't mean you can be rude or tactless. Remember: If anyone has different ideas to yours, that doesn't make them any less valid. Be honest and transparent. Nothing good comes from being dishonest. Speak your truth.

Don't put on a mask. Stop playing roles to please others. Stop faking and allow yourself to be you. The rewards are awesome. Funny enough, you will notice that the more you are yourself; the more people will be attracted to you! Try it!

Stop playing roles. Be you!

17

COMMUNICATE EFFECTIVELY

One thing successful people have in common is that they are very good communicators. They know exactly how to express their ideas, emotions, wants, wishes, hopes and disappointments. This is a considerable advantage over more introverted people or those that can't express their ideas, or don't know how to start a conversation, especially with strangers.

But no worries if you belong to the second group, this can be fixed in no time.

Here are some suggestions:

1. Stop being afraid of saying something too trivial, something inadequate or something that makes no sense at all and above all relax, because...

2. You don't need to be perfect. Stop trying. Nobody can fascinate others all the time. Be authentic and speak from the heart. People will appreciate it.

3. Its small talk. It's casual and not meant to be brilliant. It's supposed to be easy and to get the conversation going. Don't try too hard and just do it. (Hint: like everything else it gets better with practice.)

Probably the best way to start a conversation and become great at small talk is number 4:

Get your counterpart to talk about themselves. Ask questions about the others' interests like why? Where? How? For example: Where are you from? What are you doing for a living? And the family? Start the talk with questions about your counterpart and then lean back and listen...and ask some more questions. They will love you for it. In a world where everybody continually wants to talk about themselves, listening is GOLD. This is a great icebreaker, and you start your counterpart off on the one topic they are experts on...themselves.

Get others to talk about them, and they will swear you are the greatest conversationalist they ever met. Keep on asking questions, and they will say that you are one of the most interesting people they ever met.

Ask questions, and you are almost there.

18

THE DEADLY SIN IN
HUMAN RELATIONS YOU
NEED TO AVOID

Remember what I mentioned in one of the past chapters. As humans, we are innately selfish.

You are human, so you will be tempted to talk about yourself. You want to shine. You want to be admired. You want to be acknowledged. You want to impress. Anyways, you are much better off to resist this temptation. If you keep focusing the conversation on others rather than on yourself, they will have a much higher opinion of you.

One of the best preparations is always to ask yourself what you want to get out of the situation, before every meeting, phone call, or conversation. Do you want the other person's permission for something? Do you want their business? Their goodwill? If you want any of this, keep the conversation focused on them. If you only want to blow up your ego, then yes... talk about yourself all the time, but then don't expect anything else out of the conversation.

If you want to blow up your ego, be like the author who after talking for two hours about himself turned to his companion and said, 'Enough about me. Let's talk about you. What do you think about my latest book?'

If you want to be successful, let others do the talking about themselves and listen. Only talk about yourself when you are invited, or asked to do so. If others are interested in you, they will ask. If so, talk a little bit about yourself and then turn the focus back to them.

Don't be selfish. Keep the focus on them.

Part III

....

Basic Rules

19

SAY THANK YOU!

If you have read other books of mine, listened to an interview, saw me speaking or on TV, then you know that I'm a huge fan of gratitude. I think it's one of the most powerful forces in the universe and being grateful not only brings good things into our lives, but it also makes us notice more and more of those that are already there.

On our way to become people magnets and find new friends, gratitude should be one of the main ingredients. It's not enough to feel grateful and appreciative towards people and stay silent. You must show this gratitude and appreciation to everyone who deserves it.

It is human nature to like and respond to people who appreciate us and show us gratitude. Be grateful to people and show it to them with kind words or little gestures and you can be assured that it will come back to you multiplied.

The attitude of gratitude has countless benefits. If you practice it only for a couple of weeks you'll be happier, more optimistic, and more socially connected; you'll sleep better and get fewer headaches; you'll have more energy, more emotional intelligence; you'll be more forgiving, and less likely to be depressed, anxious, or lonely.

Being grateful is as great for you as for the person you are grateful to. It's worth a try, isn't it? Anyways…there are some ground rules to follow.

Once again, you have to be sincere and really mean it when you thank people. People can distinguish clearly if you are genuinely thankful or not. If it's not real, you'll have none of the benefits. Say 'Thank you' or 'I appreciate you' or 'I am glad to have you in my life' loud and clear. Say it with joy. Maintain eye contact. It means a lot more when you look people that you thank in the eyes. Say 'Thank you, Peter,' 'Thank you, Mary.'

Use people's names. It makes a huge difference.

Practice thanking people. It will change your life. If you want to become a master at thanking people don't only thank them for the obvious, thank them for the not so obvious.

So simple, yet powerful. Few things are more important than the ability to properly thank people.

Let the power of gratitude change your relationships and complete your life for the better.

20

ADMIT YOUR MISTAKES

There is nothing bad about making mistakes. You are human. Humans make mistakes. Stop feeling like a bad or useless person simply because you make mistakes every now and then.

Did you ever know somebody who had difficulties admitting their mistakes? Maybe they made up excuses and justifications—or even worse—blamed someone else for their mistake? How did it make you feel? Did it build trust with this person? Did it make you want to get to know them better and spend more time with them? I don't think so!

So, what conclusions do we draw from this? Right! If we want to build trust with people and influence them and want to be the real thing we have to find the strength of admitting our mistakes—even if it's difficult. Don't waste your energy making up excuses or justifications.

Make admitting your mistakes a habit. It's a sign of strength, and as it's not such a common trait, you will surprise people, and they might even admire you for it. Admitting a mistake and facing the consequences takes much more strength than denial. And it's much healthier. Instead of losing energy denying it, it will liberate you.

When I worked at Volkswagen in Mexico, my boss let me drive his car when I had to run an errand. (The plant is enormous. It's like a city of its own, so you get around by car.) One day, driving around and not paying attention, I hit the curbstone with the right front tyre. About three hours later my boss wanted to use his car and saw that he had a flat right front tyre. He came back into the office and told us. About four people had used his car that day. Everybody looked at the floor. I could have easily played the innocent, look into the air and done nothing. After two tense minutes, I gathered my courage and told him. 'It might have been me. I hit the curbstone.' I saw the relief on my colleagues' faces, and from looking at the floor, they were transitioning right away in making fun of me.

My boss told me, 'Well, the least you can do is help me change the tyre.' And off we went. I apologized once more to him. He was grateful that I admitted my mistake. This incident took our relationship to another level. He knew he could trust me and that I would always admit my mistakes.

Recognizing your mistakes is a sign of strength and maturity. You only have a problem if you don't learn anything from your mistakes and repeat the same mistake over and over again. If this happens, you should look at the pattern and search for the lesson and learning experience. That's it. That's all you have to do.

Admit your mistakes, but avoid repeating the same ones over and over again.

21

STOP GOSSIPING

If you want to have success in your dealings with other people, it's inevitable to let go of the toxic habit of gossiping.

I know, sometimes it's very tempting to hear the latest rumours from other people. The problem is that most probably the person who tells you these rumours starts spreading rumours about you, once you turn your back on them. But what is even worse for your reputation is what happens if you are the one spreading the dirty little stories. What if your listeners come to the same logical conclusion I have mentioned above. The worst thing that can happen to you is that they start asking themselves what you say about them behind their backs once they turn them to YOU.

So, if somebody starts gossiping in your presence, the best thing to do is to change the subject. 'Oh Charles, I'm not interested in this stuff, I'd rather hear about you! How have you been? Tell me about that last vacation of yours, you were so excited about! What else is happening in your life?' or you say 'Sorry, I really don't like talking about people who aren't present.'

Stay away from gossip and rumours as they are only harmful and destructive. Besides, they can lead to huge misunderstandings. Remember that sometimes you tell somebody a quite harmless story, and as it goes from one person to another the story changes completely and gets worse and worse. You start saying that Anne has a bad cold and at the end of the line of gossip it goes that poor Anne is on the brink of death.

Don't damage your trustworthiness and relationships by gossiping. Have sincere and profound conversations and reap the benefits further ahead.

Stop gossiping. Everybody wants to be with a person of integrity.

22

STOP JUDGING

If you want to become an influencer and make friends you have to never engage in one very toxic habit: judging and condemning others. People don't want to be judged. Period. People want to be liked, made to feel important, and appreciated. Not judged.

Put yourself in other people's shoes and walk a mile in them before you even think of judging them. Everybody we meet on our journey is fighting their own unique battle, and we have no idea what they are dealing with. Just as they have no idea what we are going through. Be kind. Show empathy. I know it's easier said than done, but on your way to be a people magnet, there is no way around it.

If there are things you don't like about other people, things that really bother you, pause a moment and reflect. Are these maybe things that bother you about yourself? Get aware of the fact that each time you're judging someone you are actually judging yourself.

Observe what most bothers you about other people. Is it, for example, that they never are on time?

I know. That's really bothering especially if YOU are always on time, right? Look a little bit closer.

Are you really always on time? Or maybe in some areas you also aren't and let people wait.

Sometimes when something bothers us about people we need to look at ourselves because we might be doing exactly those things to other people without noticing it. That's why you have people whose life is in disarray telling you, how you should live your life; people with a ton of debt telling you how to deal with your finances; overweight people telling you to eat healthier; unorganized and stressed people giving seminars on time management and organization and so on. Before judging other people, we should get our own house in order.

I try to avoid judging people as I have found myself more than once in the same situation as people that I had judged before. It was when I was in the same situation as them that I came to understand them. There's really something to the saying, 'Walk a mile (or maybe better ten) in my shoes before you judge me.'

Don't judge people. Once you are tempted to judge, take a look at yourself and see if you have the flaws you judge in other people.

23

FORGIVE EVERYONE

Have you ever been around bitter people who can't let go of the past? People who are still holding a grudge because someone did something to them a long time ago and they keep ruminating and complaining and talking about it. How is it? Do you like their company? I bet not. Remember this when YOU are in a similar situation. It's no fun to be around the complainers and the bitter ones.

The antidote to this is Forgiveness! To be a forgiving person is not only good for your relationships with other people, it's also a fast track to success and happiness.

This is not about being right or wrong; it's about you being well and not wasting energy. Forgive even if it was the other party who wronged you. You are doing it for yourself!

Being resentful or angry with people, reliving hate and anger over and over again is toxic.

It's toxic to your relationships; it's toxic to your energy; it's toxic to your health. They say being angry and having resentments towards another person is like drinking poison and hoping the other individual dies from it.

If you are not already doing it, from today onwards do yourself a huge favour and forgive everybody (including yourself). I repeat: you are not doing it for the other person; rather, you are doing it for yourself. Once you forgive and let go, you will sleep better, you will enjoy your present moments more, and a huge weight will be lifted off your shoulders.

Holding grudges never did anyone any good. It makes things worse. It's hurting you more than anybody else. Your negative feelings will hurt your health and character. Your focus will remain stuck in the past wounds, and this could attract even more unpleasant experiences into your life.

Don't misunderstand me. Forgiving others doesn't mean that you are stupid. Nor does being a forgiving person mean that people can walk over you as they please. You set clear boundaries, put limits on other's behaviour, or call them out on the spot. People who don't accept these rules or who hurt you have to go. You don't need them in your life, but do yourself one favour—don't hold grudges.

Let them go, forgive them, forget them and move on. Learn from the experience and be open to new, better adventures to come.

Don't be a fool! Forgive everyone and be fun to be around!

24

KEEP YOUR WORD

Remember a good reputation built over a long time can be destroyed in seconds. For example, by not keeping your word. If you talk a lot but don't follow up with action, people will lose trust in you. This is the worst that can happen because all personal and professional relationships are built on trust.

And it gets even worse, because you know who else will also lose trust in you? YOU! You pay a high psychological and emotional price whenever you lie, cheat, or are dishonest. Every commitment you make, even those you make to other people, is ultimately a commitment to yourself. If you don't follow through with your commitments and your promises, you are sending yourself the message 'my word is not worth anything. Hence, I'm not worth anything'.

How can you avoid this?

1. Never make promises you can't keep and over-deliver on everything you do.
2. If you say you are going to be somewhere, be there.
3. Mean everything you say. No wishy-washy talk. If you don't mean it, don't say it.
4. Do what you say you're going to do.

5. Never tell a lie. If you can't, don't or won't do something, tell people the truth right away.
6. Don't play with people's emotions.
7. Don't say things only to impress. Be authentic.

When you tell lies or when you want to impress people constantly, what you are actually transmitting to yourself is— I'M NOT GOOD ENOUGH AS I AM. I need to be someone else so that the other person will like me. That's when your self-esteem and self-confidence take a hit.

When you tell the truth, the message you communicate to yourself is that your words are worthy, your words are important. You matter. In no case should you make great promises which you can't fulfil. Don't promise greatness and then deliver mediocrity. This will damage your reputation and will repel people.

Be smart and do the opposite: under-promise and over-deliver. This will boost your value in the eyes of others, but also in the eyes of your toughest critic…yourself. People will feel great around you because you are constantly exceeding their expectations, going the extra mile every single time. A nice byproduct of this strategy is that you will also experience a lot less stress and be more relaxed.

Don't undermine your reputation and your self-worth. Tell the truth and keep your commitments.

25

TREAT OTHERS AS YOU WOULD
LIKE OTHERS TO TREAT YOU

There is one concept all religions and philosophies have in common—it was the first thing I was told twenty-five-years ago when I had started working at Disney World. It's the golden rule. 'Do unto others as you would have others do unto you.' Treat people as you want to be treated. I've followed this rule most of the time in my life. It has brought me great joy, significant relationships and probably saved me from many troubles.

Do you want to receive more compliments? Give more compliments. Do you want to be more admired? Admire more. Do you want to be loved more? Love more. Do you want recognition of your true worth? Recognize the true worth of others. Do you want sincere appreciation? Give sincere appreciation to others.

If you can give without expecting to receive anything in return, you will take your relationships to another level. Start NOW!

If the waiter brings you the wrong order in the restaurant, tell him, 'I'm sorry to trouble you, but I ordered...' I'm sure he will tell you, 'No trouble at all' and return with the right order. Why? Because you let him save his face. You showed your respect. Little phrases like, 'I'm sorry to trouble you,' 'Could you be so kind,' 'Would you mind' 'Please...' go a long, long way.

I saw a funny picture on social media a while ago. It was a price table with the following prices:

Coffee:	5.00 USD
A cup of coffee:	3.00 USD
Good morning! One cup of coffee, please:	1.00 USD

We live in a society that longs for appreciation, recognition and feeling important. The life of many people could probably be changed if only someone would make them feel important, appreciate them, and recognize their value. You can be that someone. How? When? All the time, everywhere!

As always, you have to be sincere in your appreciation, recognition and praise for other people or it won't work.

Do unto others as you would have others do unto you.

26

REMEMBER PEOPLE'S NAMES

Our name is the most significant connection to our identity and individuality. It sets us apart and makes us unique among all others. For some, it's even the most important word in their world.

Yet most of us don't remember names. Many times because we are so busy rehearsing what to say next that we forget the name of the person we had just met. We don't take the time to concentrate and fix the name in our mind through repetition. No worries. You are not alone. It even happens to me! I'm learning as I'm writing this book and at the end of this chapter you will know why remembering people's names is so important and what benefits it will bring you.

So, why should we remember people's names? First of all, using someone's name when interacting with them is one of the simplest and most profound secrets of success. Why? Because we show people that we care about them. We care about them enough to remember their name. It is a sign of courtesy and a way of recognizing them. Don't underestimate this even if it seems to be so unbelievably basic and simple.

When you remember a person's name the next time you meet them, you will make quite a lasting impression on them, because you will show them they were important enough for you to remember their name. This could be the start of something special because this person now always positively associates you. You remembered their name. You made them feel important and respected.

Dale Carnegie was right. Our name is the sweetest and most important sound in our ears. Every time someone mentions it in a conversation it makes us feel good (if the conversation is positive that is), it makes us turn towards the speaker, and it gives us a boost of happiness and the feeling of 'He/she did it again. They mentioned my name again I must be important!' (If this is just me, please let me know... I might have to have a look at it.)

How do you feel when somebody mentions your name? Important, right? Every time you say the name of a person you charge them with a series of positive feelings, and at the end of the conversation, they most probably will feel positively connected to you. The most charismatic people are always described as making the person they are talking to feel like the most important person in the world. How are they doing it? They are using this person's name frequently, and they are asking questions: 'So tell me, John, what brought you here.' 'That's very interesting John.' 'Excuse me for a second John, I just saw my friend Barney over there.'

Try using names everywhere. In the supermarket or in the shops. Remember the name of the waitress, the cleaning women and of the senior executive and see what it does. Probably magic!

Remember people's names. You'll make people feel more important, and most importantly, you build better relationships and trust.

27

AVOID ARGUMENTS

Do you ever really, really win an argument? Yes? I don't think so. You might have 'won' the argument, but you surely have lost your 'opponents' sympathy. Is proving somebody wrong making them like you? Sometimes, it's better to maintain peace and harmony than to be right. You don't really win anything by being a know-it-all. You only make people feel uncomfortable and, in the worst case, lose their face. Remember: This is a book about making friends and influencing people. Arguments, knowing everything better than your peers, ridiculing people have no place in it.

Avoid arguments. 99 per cent of all arguments end with each of the parties being even more convinced that they are right. As I said before: You can't win an argument. If you lose it, you lose it; if you win it, you also lose it. Why? Because you have made the other party look inferior and might even have hurt their dignity. And yes. You probably haven't changed their opinion anyway.

How many times did you win an argument with your boss? Did the promotion come right away, or are you still waiting? How many times did you win an argument against a client? Were you right? Yes? Did you win? Yes? Did he buy? Probably not. If possible, concentrate on things you agree on instead of focusing on things on which you differ.

If someone wants to start an argument with you, agree with them. The blue car is better than the red one? Yes! You are right. Period. No room for an argument. It's not a sign of weakness to avoid arguments. It's a sign of strength. Remember, you can't win anyway. If you argue and contradict, you might win an argument now and then, but it's a sour victory because you will never get your opponents' goodwill. And which do you prefer? A victory or a person's goodwill?

Have you noticed that the more you argue with a person, the more stubborn they become? People want to feel important, and as long as you argue with them about a matter, some people get this feeling of importance. So, instead of wasting your time arguing with them, give them the feeling of significance and win their goodwill. Arguments are resolved by putting yourself in the other person's shoes, honestly, trying to see things from their viewpoint.

Avoid arguments. Save your time. You can't afford to lose time arguing, nor can you afford to take the consequences.

So when you disagree with someone, remember the following things so as not to let it turn into an argument.

Control your temper and listen. Let the other party talk and don't interrupt. Are there any parts where you agree? Be honest. Apologize for your mistakes. This will surprise your opponent—remember not many people are able to admit mistakes. Promise to study your opponent's ideas and think them over and thank them for their time and feedback. Be sincere.

Ask yourself the following questions: Could they be right? What benefit will my reaction have? What price do I have to pay if I'm right? Is it better to be quiet? Where is the opportunity here?

Avoid arguments. You can't win them.

Part IV

....

Lead by Example

28

PRAISE AND ACKNOWLEDGE
PEOPLE HONESTLY AND SINCERELY

Praise and acknowledgment are basic needs of people. We need to feel important; we are craving for appreciation. Remember how you feel when someone praises you or gives you a compliment. Remember how it brightens up your moment, afternoon, day and even sometimes your week. Mark Twain said that he could live for two weeks on a good compliment, and so can I. What about you?

Studies prove that teams with managers that acknowledge and praise their work are up to 31 per cent more productive. Companies that have a work environment based on acknowledgment and praise multiply their benefits.

We don't even need studies for it. Just remember how you feel. And now I'm going to tell you a secret: Others will feel exactly as you do. Never let kind words go to waste by not saying them. Tell people the kind things you would love to hear. Don't spare with praise and acknowledgment as it does miracles—and it's completely free. It doesn't cost you a thing to say nice words to others.

So, from now on, go through life looking for someone and something to praise and then do it.

Just have in mind that the praise has to be sincere. If it's not sincere, don't give it. Praise the behaviour, not the person. It will create an incentive for others to act the same way.

Examples:

'Your work is excellent' rather than 'You are a great guy.'

'Your art is simply beautiful' rather than 'you are a good artist.'

Praising and acknowledging people has a remarkable side effect—it makes all individuals involved, happy. The receiver and the giver by praising and acknowledging you are actually doing something good for yourself! Seeing the happiness and gratitude you bring to others by adopting this habit will make you feel incredibly good.

Make saying kind things to at least three different people a daily habit.

29

SHOW EVERYONE KINDNESS AND RESPECT

Show every person you meet kindness and respect. Every person has a story as compelling and complicated as your own. Just as you are extraordinary, so are they.

Give them a fair chance to interact with you. Don't make the mistake of judging or discarding them right away. You can learn something from everybody you meet on the journey of your life.

Many times in my life, people I had first thought of as 'What a strange person' or 'He doesn't seem to be very bright' have become my best friends. Meet people with kindness and respect and great things can come from it.

Every now and then you might end up disappointed when you are kind to people, and they don't respond to it, or maybe even take advantage of you. Don't let this change you. It's not your problem; it's theirs. It's a price worth paying for meeting all the other great people who'll come into your life.

Even the rude people you meet deserve your kindness and respect. Well, actually it's them who probably need your kindness most. Remember, if somebody is rude to you, it's their problem, not yours.

Bear in mind that 'what goes around comes around.' If you treat people with patience and respect and are nice to them, you will attract nice people into your life in the long-term.

One good trick I learned a long time ago when I was a waiter at Disney World in Orlando, Florida is that if somebody was rude to me, I became nicer and nicer to them, and the more offensive they got, the nicer I became. It worked. In 99 per cent of the cases, I ended up winning their sympathy. They were not used to this because usually, they get their energy from people who get defensive and become angry with them.

The best way to show rude people your teeth is to smile at them.

Show everyone kindness and respect. They deserve it. Even the 'bad' ones.

30

DON'T GIVE DIRECT ORDERS— BE MORE SUBTLE

People don't like to be given direct orders. It goes against our nature. You can convince people much more subtly by asking questions like 'Did you consider this option?' or 'Do you think that would work?' or 'What would you think of this?', 'Maybe this one would work better?'

Always give people the opportunity to get things done themselves. Let them come to their own solutions; let them learn from their mistakes. That's how it sticks. It has the positive side effect that it doesn't make a person lose face and maintains their feeling of being important. This kind of treatment of people will encourage their cooperation instead of going against you. It will also avoid resentment and anger.

Asking questions is not only a smoother way to get results it also stimulates the creativity of the person you ask questions. It's much easier for people to accept a decision or an order if they at least feel that they had their part in the process.

Often if you have a challenge, it's a much better way to explain it to your employees, friends or family than to give out strict orders. If you ask people, they come up with the best solutions. Use that potential.

Effective leaders use the power questions technique instead of giving direct orders.

31

BELIEVE IN PEOPLE'S POTENTIAL

If one of your employees or team members suddenly doesn't perform anymore, you can threaten him, which only causes resentment and maybe further suffering of his performance or you can even fire him, but that doesn't really solve anything, right? It will cost you three times his or her year's salary to onboard, train and get a new employee to his level. A friend of mine who is a successful businessman, in this case, invites his employees for a heart-to-heart talk. He tells his employees that he was pleased with their performance, but he noted some performance drop and asks what he can do to help. How can we solve this problem together?

If you want to improve a specific skill in a person act as if he or she already had that particular skill.

Goethe already knew this hundreds of years ago: 'If we treat people as they ought to be, we help them become what they are capable of becoming.'

Remind your employees of their outstanding work in the past, give them a vision of themselves they are eager to live up to, believe in them, and they will rise to the occasion. It works. It's not magic. It's the Pygmalion Effect—Our belief in a person's potential brings that potential to life.

See them as if they already had the trait, talk to them as if they already had the trait. Let the Pygmalion Effect work for you and you will see miracles happen.

When Robert Rosenthal and his team went to an elementary school in the late sixties and did some intelligence tests on the students, they told the teachers that students A, B, and C had extraordinary results and were academic superstars. The teachers could not mention this to the students, nor treat them differently, and to make them understand the seriousness of the project, they were even told that they were being observed.

At the end of the year, the tests were repeated and, to no one's surprise, A, B, and C posted off-the-chart intellectual ability again. Again? Well, the fun thing was that the researchers had lied to the teachers the first time around. When tested the first time A, B, and C were absolutely ordinary and randomly picked by the researchers. They concluded that the mere belief of the teacher in the potential of the students brought that potential to life.

You can easily lead people and make them trust you if you have their respect and you earn that respect by believing in them and showing respect for their abilities and their work.

Remember that the Pygmalion Effect can happen anywhere. The expectations you have about your co-workers, your children, your friends, and spouses—whether or not they are ever mentioned—can turn that expectation into reality.

Believe in the potential of people, and you will see miracles happen.

32

BE AN EXAMPLE

We are continually influencing the actions and attitudes of other people, not only of those we come in contact with but also of their spouses, kids, and colleagues. So, the question is in which direction will we influence them? The best way of influencing others is by being an example. Treat other people how you want to be treated. Adopt the attitude you want other people to show you. You might have heard the theory that other persons are like a mirror towards us. Observe this fact closely!

Tal Ben-Shahar once told this story about a mother who with her son came to see Gandhi for some advice. The mother told Gandhi, 'Please, tell my son to eat less sugar.' Gandhi watched both of them and after a moment of silence told the mother. 'Come back in one month.' The mother was astonished as she was keen on Gandhi talking to her son, but followed his order.

Four weeks later they came back. Once it was their turn, Gandhi looked at the kid and said, 'Son. You really need to eat less sugar.' The mother looked at him and said, 'Master, it has been such a long trip and we had to travel a long time twice to see you. Why couldn't you say that a month ago? I don't understand.' And Gandhi said, 'Because a month ago, I was eating too much sugar.'

The best way to change people is to change them by your example. Don't tell your partner to go to the gym and lose some weight. Go to the gym and lose some weight. Don't tell your employees to take every phone call, while you don't pick up the phone. You take every phone call first. If you are a boss 'prescribing' company training for your employees you should be the first one participating in that training. When your employees see that you are serious about change they will get serious, too.

You need to accept that you cannot change others. What you can do is to accept them as they are and be the best example and a person that you can be. Instead of complaining about your partner, colleagues, or spouse, be the best colleague or spouse possible. Not satisfied with your employees? Be the best boss possible! When you shift from 'others have to change' to 'what if I change, maybe then the others also change' everything will change.

Be the example of what you want to see in the world.

33

REMAIN HUMBLE

Remain humble. While some people in our ego-driven world think that humble persons are weak and passive and are completely lacking of self-respect; science and religious scholars agree that humility is a virtue and character strength.

Most of the time, when we look closely at this, we notice that the majority of successful people in business and sports, in reality, have remained humble. Who would you rather spend your time with? A person who is successful but remains humble or an arrogant braggart?

Humble people have a clear idea of their abilities and achievements; they acknowledge their flaws and admit mistakes and limitations. They are open to new ideas even if they don't entirely agree with them. They appreciate the value of everything and accept that there are many different ways that people can contribute to this world.

Studies show that humble people are more admired and that most people see the character trait of humility as positive. In one study, humble teachers were rated as more effective and humble lawyers were rated as more likeable by jurors. In another survey, more than 80 per cent of the participants indicated that it's important that professionals demonstrate modesty and humility in their work.

In this book, *Gratitude Works* (pp.124) Robert Emmons shows us twenty humble practices in daily life practiced by Paul Wong. They are the following. You will see many of the principles we talked about in this book:

- Acknowledging your wrongdoing
- Receiving correction and feedback graciously
- Refraining from criticizing others
- Forgiving others who have wronged us
- Apologizing to others, we have wronged
- Enduring unfair treatments with patience and forgiving spirit
- Thinking and speaking about the good things of other people
- Rejoicing over other people's success
- Counting our blessings for everything, good and bad
- Seeking opportunities to serve others
- Being willing to remain anonymous in helping others
- Showing gratitude for our successes
- Giving due credit to others for our successes
- Treating success as a responsibility to do more for others
- Being willing to learn from our failures
- Assuming responsibility for our failures
- Accepting our limitations and circumstances
- Accepting the social reality of discrimination and prejudice
- Treating all people with respect regardless of their social status
- Enjoying the lowly status of being an outsider and a nobody

Remain humble and enjoy the advantages of it.

34

LET THE OTHER PERSON COME UP
WITH YOUR IDEA

Let's talk about ideas. Which ones do you find better, the ones you come up with, or the ones that people want to convince you of? If you are like most people, you will prefer the first option—coming up with your own ideas. Well, surprise, surprise, so does everybody else. No one likes being sold on something or being told something. We want to feel that the decision was ours or that the idea was ours. We want people to ask us for our opinions, our wishes, and our thoughts. So, why not use this to your advantage?

The best way is always to plant the idea in somebody's mind and let them think about it and to meditate on it. Frequently, you will see the same person coming up with the same idea a couple of days later defending it as if it were their own idea. (I have to admit that this happens to me from time to time).

The easiest way to let the other person feel it was their idea is ASKING. When you make an offer, ask the client what he really needs, or ask them to complete your offer to themselves. If you go on a family vacation, ask your family where they want to go and come to a consensus. If you are going out with friends, ask them what they like best. If you are going on a date night with your spouse ask him or her, what they'd like to do. So easy and yet so difficult, right?

Ask and let the other person come up with your idea.

35

BE ON TIME

On your way to becoming a master of human relations don't you ever underestimate small courtesies such as being on time for an appointment.

Punctuality is a sign of discipline and respect for others. Without it, you might come across as slightly offensive, even if you are the nicest person in the world. If I haven't convinced you yet, bear the following French proverb in mind: 'The while we keep a man waiting, he reflects on our shortcomings.' True or true?

Of course, there are cultural differences. For example, in Mexico and Spain people are very relaxed about punctuality, but in Germany not being punctual is seen as being highly unprofessional and might ruin your chances in any endeavour. A friend of mine lost a multiple 100,000 Dollar business opportunity because he showed up 15 minutes too late for a business appointment with a German company. While in some cultural circles unpunctuality can be seen as 'I'll be late so that you can see how important I am', others will see it as disrespectful and not forgive you.

Be punctual! You don't even have to do it to be exceptionally polite; but instead, you're actually doing it for yourself. I would even recommend you to arrive ten minutes early. This will already give you a head start in any meeting or negotiation. Why? Because you can use those ten minutes to relax and prepare. You can compose your thoughts and get used to the environment instead of arriving in a rush.

When I started being punctual—or better said, arriving ten minutes early—I noticed that those ten minutes made me feel a lot better and gave me a lot of peace of mind. I felt very relaxed. I also felt very comfortable, professional, and polite. In fact, I now feel uncomfortable when I arrive just in time. Try it for yourself and see if it adds to your life or not!

Be on time and enjoy the benefits of it.

36

FOCUS ON THE OTHER
PERSON'S STRENGTHS

Did we already talk about the power of focus? It's one of the most decisive influences of your daily life. Have you ever thought about buying a new car and then saw precisely that type of car everywhere? Have you or your spouse been pregnant, and suddenly pregnant women seemed to be everywhere? Or you had a cast, and suddenly everyone seemed to have a cast? When we look for something, we see it everywhere. This is called selective perception. Your focus is essential because science shows that how we experience our life is a matter of interpretation, a matter of choice, and it's up to us where we choose to put our focus.

Our focus creates our reality, so we see more of what we focus on. In one phrase: Our focus determines our overall perception of the world.

So, if we focus on other people's strengths what will happen? Yes. Exactly. We'll see more of their strengths! Will that improve our personal relationships? You bet it will.

This is a magic cure for all our relationships. Imagine focusing on the strengths of your spouse instead of nagging?

Suddenly, you will see all the great things you fell in love with in the first place. Or your employees? Suddenly, you'll be able to see their full potential instead of their weaknesses and faults.

Look at other persons in a new way:

- What are their unique strengths?
- What are you most proud of thinking about them?
- What do they do best?
- What are their most significant personal and professional accomplishments?
- What gifts do they have?
- What makes them unique and compelling?

Take this a step further. What would happen if we concentrated on our similarities rather than our differences? Exactly. We'd see a lot more of what we have in common.

Would that be great for our world? You bet.

That's undoubtedly a much better foundation to come to agreements with than focusing on our differences, right? In all conflicts or negotiations, the most essential ingredient is to have a common goal—if not, they fail. So, from now on, focus on similarities. What can be the common goal?

Focus on the other person's strengths and see them in an entirely new way.

Part V

....

If You Have to Say it,
Say it Smoothly

37

DON'T CRITICIZE

Criticism is useless. The only thing it does is put a person on the defensive and makes them try to justify themselves. Criticism is dangerous. It hurts the pride of a person and causes resentment. It's proven that we learn more, become better and more productive when our good behaviour is praised and acknowledged, than if we get punished and work under pressure. A critical comment just before an important presentation in the likes of 'Pete, this is very important for us. Don't screw it up like last time,' can set the person up for failure, while encouragement and praising the strengths of a person like 'John, I admire how you prepare these presentations. Go and knock it out of the park', can seal the deal.

The thought that criticism can improve something is old and outdated. Criticism only brings resentment and can demoralize family members, friends, colleagues, and employees.

The best thing you can do is to think really hard if your critique is necessary. You know for sure that it won't be any good. So, the best thing is to take some deep breaths or leave the room. Be especially careful with e-mails as once they are sent, there's no way to get them back. Not like in the old days when you wrote letters and you at least had the chance to get it out of the mail before the damages were done. Every now and then, when I write an angry mail, I decide not to send it and leave it as a draft overnight. If I still want to send it the next day I send it, but in 99 per cent of the cases, I don't. The anger is out of my system, and I go on with more important work.

We all know people we want to lecture, improve, and change, but you know what? Forget it. It's impossible to change other people unless they are the ones who want to change. What you can do is start with yourself. Be the change you want to see in others, be the role model; be the example.

Only small minds criticize because they are either cowards, or too weak to create something themselves, or both.

No good will come out of criticizing others. Swallow your criticism and work on yourself instead.

38

HOW TO CRITICIZE PEOPLE CONSTRUCTIVELY

We talked about it in the last chapter. The best thing is to not criticize at all. Anyway every now and then you might have no other choice. It's a very sensitive subject. First let me ask you a question: Do you like it when people criticize you? Be honest! Okay, I go first:

I don't like it at all. And guess what: most of the people you cross paths with are like you and me. They also don't like being criticized. I know…we can learn from the critics blah blah blah. I prefer learning without being criticized, though. Anyway, we have to look at it so if we ever get tempted to criticize someone we at least do it the right way. If you criticize people to put them in their place, to tell them off or to prove that you are better than them, you better stop right now. Then my friend you are at the wrong place because this book is written to make friends, not to get rid of them and that's what harsh criticism will do.

It will only cause resentment and bad vibrations.

There are ways to give constructive criticism. Let's leave the word criticism out of it and call it feedback. Feedback is supposed to help people, to correct them, to let them know how other people can perceive what they're doing. Well-intended feedback goes a long way in influencing people.

Here are some golden rules:

1. If you have to criticize, do it in absolute privacy behind closed doors. Don't raise your voice and nobody should be listening. Adhere to the easy rule of thumb 'Praise in public, criticize in private.' Unfortunately, even today too many people do it the other way round. They criticize in public and praise in private—if they praise at all, and that ruins their relationships, both the professional and personal ones.

2. Start with praise. If you have to criticize start pointing out what the person is doing very well, then drop your critique point and if you a very swift guy or gal close with another praise. This is also called the sandwich method.

3. Always criticize the behaviour and never ever the person.

4. Provide solutions. Find out together with the person you give feedback to what would be the right way to do things. When you are telling them what they are doing wrong, also let them know how they can do it right.

5. Don't demand cooperation. Nicely ask for it. It's a fact that people are more willing to cooperate with you if you ask them nicely than if you demand it. Demanding should only be a measure of last resort.

6. Just say it once—if possible. If it happened only once, don't repeat it over and over again. If it happens over and over again, you might have a problem...

7. As I said before: Finish the feedback session on a friendly

note, point out what the person is doing well and finish with praise.

8. Watch your body language and tone of voice. In a study, people who received negative feedback with a positive body language (a smile) and a nice tone of voice felt a lot better afterwards, than people who received positive feedback with a negative body language and a harsh tone of voice. Can you believe that? So much about the power of body language and the tonality of our voice. I don't want to imagine how I'd feel if someone delivered negative feedback with a negative body language and a negative tone of voice...

Don't criticize unless you absolutely have to. If you have to, follow the aforementioned rules.

39

HANDLE COMPLAINTS SMOOTHLY

Do you know the best way to handle complaints? Let the other person do the talking. They are a valuable source of information. Don't get all defensive. People simply want their complaints handled and the problem solved. They value the care and attention given to them.

So, the best thing is to let them do the talking. Ask them lots of questions and even when you are tempted to interrupt, keep listening profoundly and patiently. Encourage them to let it all out. Give them space to blow some steam off if they need to. Repeat their points back to them to make sure you have understood them right. They talk, you listen. The relation should be 80:20 or even 90:10. Show them that you can see things from their perspective and that you only want a solution that makes them happy. If you made mistakes admit them and apologize for them.

Accompany the conversation with a positive body language like visual contact, nodding your head, showing that you are interested. You can even make notes while you are listening. Above all, keep listening—don't disconnect even if they are telling you things you don't like to hear. When it's your turn to speak, speak clearly and in a simple language.

Complaints can be a great resource for future improvements. Where did mistakes happen? What went wrong? What would they do? How would they like to solve the complaint? What do they want? Don't jump to conclusions and search for solutions, not obstacles. Use the other person's feedback for future actions. That's all there is. Easy isn't it?

If somebody complains, you listen.

40

A GREAT WAY TO GIVE FEEDBACK

People don't like to be criticized, but of course, we can't tip around others on our toes the whole time, so when the time for honest feedback comes, some also call it 'constructive criticism'. Here's, how to go about it. It's also called the 'sandwich method' or 'the feedback sandwich.'

Start with something pleasant, a compliment, positive attributes, what you like about the person. Then you tell them about the behaviour, actions they can improve, and you close again on a positive note pointing out another thing you like very much about their performance or their behaviour.

Also, be diplomatic when you come to the critical point, maybe some mistakes the person makes. Don't call them mistakes. Be diplomatic and say 'if there is anything to improve it could be…', 'there are some things you could do even better.'

If you learn to start your conversations pointing out the positive in the other person and also closing on a positive note your relationships at home and work will improve a lot. Nobody wants to be around a nagging wife or husband or will do the best work for the ever-criticizing boss. Try out the feedback sandwich, and you'll see miraculous changes.

You will get much further with the feedback sandwich

than the 'hammer method' will ever take you.

Last but not least a very important thing: Don't use the word 'but.' The word 'but' cancels out everything that stands before it. If you say 'I'm pleased with the way you handle our customers, BUT...' chances are that the receiver of the feedback won't care about any of the praise that came before the 'BUT,' and will only stay with the criticism that comes after the 'BUT'. The feedback will lose its effectivity and maybe even credibility. You can easily avoid this by using 'and' instead of 'but.'

Begin giving feedback with praise and honest appreciation.

41

LET THE OTHER PERSON
SAVE FACE

This is of immense importance when talking about human relationships, yet very few of us ever think about it. We are so good at ignoring other people's feelings, criticizing others in front of their peers, getting our way, yes even threatening without ever thinking about the damage we are doing, hurting the other person's pride and identity. Stopping for a few seconds, putting ourselves in the other person's shoes, being a bit more considerate would avoid all the damage done.

In just a few short moments, we can destroy relationships if we are inconsiderate and don't let the other person save face. How many good people leave their companies, because they don't get along with their boss or colleagues? I'm sure you know the saying 'People don't change jobs, they change bosses.'

When somebody makes a mistake, let them save face. Don't destroy the relationship or even the person. Instead be encouraging, tell them it's normal to make mistakes and show them you have confidence in them. This can do miracles and instead of losing the person and watch their performance dwindle you just might have boosted this person's performance because he or she wants to live up to the high hopes you have in them.

Let the other person save face.

42

MAKE PEOPLE FEEL HAPPY ABOUT WHAT YOU ARE TELLING THEM TO DO

We don't like to be told what to do. Period. Even if it's from people close to us. The trick is to make people happy about what you are telling them to do or not to do. If you choose somebody else to do a job tell the person who is unhappy about the fact that they are too important to do this job, or that you have a better future project for them in hand. Same goes if you offer them a task that they might not find valuable. Let them honestly feel that they are essential and that you are delighted that they're accepting this task. Let them feel that they are doing you a favour.

Try this technique also with your children or spouse.

A brilliant way of rejecting offers or invitations is this one:

1. Express gratitude for the invitation
2. Show your honest regret that you can't accept the job or the event
3. Suggest a substitute who can do the job instead of you

This doesn't even give the other party time to be unhappy

about your refusal but changes their perspective to some other person who could accept the job.

A technique often used is to make up and give titles to people. The great emperor, Napoleon himself applied this technique creating a 'Legion of Honour,' naming his Generals 'Marshals of France' and his troops 'The great Army.' In companies, we often see this technique when managers lose power but are 'praised' into positions with a better sounding title (and a lower salary).

As I mentioned many times in this book, you need to be sincere. Be empathic. Don't make false promises and concentrate on the benefits for the other person. You need to know what you want the other person to do. Don't give orders. Convince the person how they will benefit from accomplishing the task. This goes without saying, but I'll still mention it: Instead of saying 'Peter, do this, this and this', say 'Peter if you could do this and this it would really make us look great in the meeting / in front of the customer' etc. It will make all the difference.

Of course, it would be naïve to think that you will always get a favourable reaction to this approach. That just won't happen, but you are much more likely to change someone's attitude this way than by threatening, harsh orders or other kinds of pressure. Start trying it and let me know how it works for you.

Don't tell people what to do. Make them happy about what you are telling them to do.

43

WATCH YOUR BODY LANGUAGE

Your body doesn't lie. You can try to control your gestures, you can say one thing and mean another but sooner, or later your body will give you away. If you say it's great and don't mean it, observers might see your head shaking while you should nod. Whole books have been written about the power of body language. You can use your body language actually to feel more confident or to go from sadness to happiness. Although the fact that your body language and tone of voice are much more important than the words you are transmitting—words 7 per cent, tone 13 per cent and body language 80 per cent—have turned out to be a myth, there is still something to it. For example as we mentioned before, people who were criticized by a happy-looking boss felt better afterward than people praised by an angry-looking boss.

In this chapter, we will look at one easy trick to build trust in no time: Mirroring. Mirroring the other person's body language. Mirroring means you adjust some aspects of your own body language to the body language of your companion. For example, if they lean forward, you lean forward, if the incline their head to the right, you incline your head to the right. You move like the other person moves and mirror their body language. Yup.

This works amazingly because you directly communicate with the other person's subconscious mind. You're telling the person 'Look I'm like you and I agree with your points of view.' When you mirror people, you make them feel comfortable. Just a couple of warnings: Don't exaggerate it, don't start imitating people right away and don't use it to manipulate people.

You will notice that with people you get along well, like your best friend, or your parents, this works automatically. In Neurolinguistic Programming and Coaching this is called 'Building Rapport.'

Here are some ways to build rapport. You can mirror the following things:

- The whole body
- Part of the body
- The upper or lower body
- Head angles, shoulders
- The changes of voice like tone, volume speed, the way of emphasizing
- The language the other person uses
- Facial expressions
- Gestures
- Repetitive phrases
- Breathing rhythm

Also, you can do exactly the opposite of what the person does to take the lead. Like talking slower when they are excited. Uncross your arms when their arms are crossed. This is also a way to confirm if real rapport is happening. If the other person after a while follows your body movements, you have connected.

Try this and practice it and you will see great things happening in your relationships with other people.

44

RECOGNIZE THE WORTH OF EVERY INDIVIDUAL

If you fail to recognize the personal worth of others, you will run into a whole lot of trouble. It's the beginning of the end of all human relationships. Out of it comes divorce, quarrels or leaving one's work. You know that people don't leave jobs, they leave bad bosses.

The most common mistakes that damage relationships are the following:

- Failure to give credit for suggestions
- Failure to correct unfairness
- Failure to praise and encourage
- Criticizing people in front of others
- Failure to ask employees their opinions
- Failure to inform employees of their progress
- Favouritism

Make people feel worthy by thinking that they are important. Yes, it's that easy. If you are convinced that other people are important, your behaviour will show it.

Remember, people want to feel important. If they think they are important, they will feel worthy. You can influence that. You can make people feel worthy by thinking and showing them that they are important. When you consider somebody to be important, you will reflect that thinking in your vocal language, body language and everything you do.

Notice people. Everybody wants to be noticed. When you notice somebody, you are paying them a big compliment. You're boosting their morale showing them 'I recognize you.' And what happens then? People become friendlier, more helpful and better workers.

Don't compete with people. There's no need for that. If someone tells you of some great things they have done, don't tell them of something even greater that you have done. Just show your genuine interest and let them know that you are impressed by them. If you tell them that they influence or inspire you, you will have won an ally for life. They will probably think you are one of the smartest and kindest people they have ever met.

If you start competing with them, they will only think that you are an idiot who doesn't have any idea what he's talking about. Competition is an unnecessary waste of time that doesn't have any benefits at all.

Recognize the worth of every individual, and you will win allies for life.

45

TALK ABOUT YOUR OWN
MISTAKES FIRST

If you really, really have to criticize someone—remember we said don't criticize at all if you can avoid it somehow, if not—a proper technique is to talk about your own mistakes first.

Before you start calling someone out for their mistakes, put yourself in their shoes. Didn't you make the same mistakes—or even worse—when you were their age, when you were new at your job, or when you did something the first time?

Maybe the person you criticize is actually doing much better at the job than you were at the same age or time. It's a lot easier to listen to a person criticizing you if this person first admits that they also make mistakes and that they are far from perfect.

Another useful technique is humbling yourself and praising the other person first before you mention their faults. Who can get mad at you for criticizing them if you first praise them? You might even turn this person into a loyal fan and friend. Humility and praise do work wonders even today.

Admit your mistakes—even if you haven't corrected them yet—this makes you an authentic, honest person that people want to be around, because you are of a rare breed. In the best case, you can even convince somebody to change their behaviour and not make the same mistakes you made.

Talk about your mistakes first and praise a lot, and people will want to hear your opinion and advice.

Part VI

....

Multiply Your Influence with These Habits

46

BE NICE

If you want to make friends, be liked, and influence people, there is a very simple recipe for that: be nice. Yup. It's that easy. Forget about old beliefs like 'Good guys always finish last.' Forget your fear that people will cheat you and run over you if you are nice. Yes. It can happen. It's happened to me many times. It doesn't matter. In the end, you win. I'd rather take the risk that other people will take advantage of me every now and then, than miss out on all the great people I met BECAUSE I chose to be a nice guy. You know, in the real world good guys (and girls) actually finish first.

That doesn't mean that you have to let other people get the better of you. If you notice that people are abusing your goodwill, confront them and ban them from your life. They will be the ones missing out.

My friend Manuel is the nicest guy you can imagine. Always helping, always smiling, people like to be around him. He has an immensely powerful network that he uses to help everyone, but when he notices people taking advantage of him, he tells them very clearly that they can now leave his inner circle and if they do any more bad stuff he will use the same network to destroy them. In his words, 'Marc, I'm the nicest guy to nice people, but—even though I hate it—if somebody is bad to me, I'm worse. If somebody is rude to me, I'm ruder. If somebody disrespects me, I'm even more disrespectful.' I have never seen this side of him. And I never will. Because I'm nice.

Being nice will pay you dividends in the long-term. Remember 'what goes around comes around.' Do everything you can to empower people. See the greatness in them. If you can see their greatness, you are actually contributing to that greatness. Your belief in the potential of a person awakens this potential.

Every time you meet someone, try and see the greatness that lies in this person. Everybody has something unique they are great at. Ask yourself 'What makes them special? What's their gift?'

As you focus on it, you will discover it. It also makes you more tolerant of not-so-friendly people. You can say 'I'm sure they have great qualities, and today they only have a bad day…'

Be nice but don't let other people fool you. Even nice people also say 'NO' or 'enough is enough' every now and then.

47

BE POSITIVE

Who do you like being around more? An optimist who always has a solution for every problem or a pessimist, who has a problem for every solution!

You are reading this book, so I guess you like being more around optimists, right?

Well, guess what. So does anybody else—or at least most people.

Do you want to be a people magnet? Be positive. Irradiate positive vibrations wherever you go, smile a lot. See solutions. People will love to be around you.

The best is optimism can be learned. It's not a matter of genes. The only difference between an optimist and a pessimist is how they interpret events. Pessimists interpret events as permanent and personal—'what's wrong with me?', 'I'll never learn.' Optimists see events as temporary. 'I wasn't in good shape today; I'm sure I'll do better tomorrow. Nevertheless, I'm one step closer to the goal.'

Some see failure as a catastrophe and give up; others see it as an opportunity for growth and success.

Nonetheless, there are even more benefits to being an optimist. Optimists are generally more successful; their biological and psychological immune system is stronger...they even live longer. (Please don't take this as an excuse to live an unhealthy lifestyle. If you smoke forty cigarettes a day, being an optimist might not help a lot.)

Be an optimist. Lift people's spirit up when they come to you. Not in a false way. We've already learned that false doesn't go very far. Same with optimism. False optimism sooner or later leads to disillusion, anger and hopelessness. Be a 'realistic optimist' who knows that positive thinking alone is not enough. You also have to add optimism, passion and hard work to the success formula.

Be an optimist. Be positive in every interaction. It's free, and people will seek your company.

48

PRAISE AND PRAISE A LOT!

Praise and acknowledgment can go a long way. Recently, some fantastic studies about the power of praise have been published. We always knew it, but now we have the numbers. People who are praised four times a quarter tend to stay longer at their jobs and perform a lot better. This can save a company hundreds of thousands of dollars. Many times when we ask people about their best day at work, they will tell us about a day their boss praised them.

But it goes even further. Praise can change a person's life. Dale Carnegie writes in his classic, *How to make friends and influence people* about how praise altered the future of H.G. Wells from being suicidal to becoming one of the great American novelists and one of the fathers of science fiction, or how Lawrence Tibbet went from singing in a church choir and hardly getting by to becoming a famous opera singer and recording artist. Both of these great artists' stories were changed by a little bit of praise, by some small encouragement.

Use the power of praise. Praise the slightest improvements. Inspire everyone you come in contact with to use the hidden talents they possess. You'll inspire the other person to keep improving. When I look back at my life, I find moments where some words of praise have changed my whole future. I'm sure the same thing happened to you. Many times, it is the praise of our parents that keeps us going when others already had discarded us. It's said that Enrico Caruso, the most celebrated opera singer of his time, was told that he couldn't sing, while his mother encouraged him and praised his voice.

If you start praising people for what they do well—instead of constantly reminding them of their faults—you will see true miracles happening. They will capitalize on that praise, and more and more of their mistakes will disappear. It's the same effect that you achieve when you concentrate on your strengths. Praise a person, and you awake their desire to excel. They will do everything they can to live up to the high opinion you have of them. See people's potential, praise them for it, and you'll help them to awaken and grow that potential.

When you praise, go into details. 'Good job' is not enough. Tell the person exactly what he or she is doing well and why it's so crucial for you or your company. Remember, we all want real appreciation and praise, but it has to be sincere and genuine. The principles in this book only work when they are honest and come directly from your heart.

Transform people's lives by praising them.

49

HOW TO MAKE A GOOD IMPRESSION

Remember that you have about 3 seconds to make a good first impression. Your very first words and actions will set the tone for the entire encounter. So, start your conversations on a positive note. A life-changing trick is to ask yourself before any meeting or phone call, 'What do I want from this?'

Are you worried about what others will think of you? Welcome to the club. Most people are. I have good news for you though. How you are perceived is in your power. Other people form their opinion of you mainly from the opinion you have about yourself. If you are not perceived as you would like, have a look inside yourself. What can you do? How do you perceive yourself? How would you want to be perceived? Start acting the way you would like to be perceived.

Be authentic. We already talked about it before. If you are trying to be someone else, you are subconsciously telling yourself 'I'm not good enough' and you are transmitting this to your surroundings. Value everything. Yourself, your job, your family, others. The more value you give yourself and others, the more others will think of you—remember it has to be sincere, if it's not it will backfire. Don't knock the competition or other people down to look better. Those times are gone. It damages your reputation. Boost your strengths and productivity. Be so good the others can't ignore you.

Keep the conversation optimistic. Nobody wants to be with a complainer and be confident that people will like you—at least 50 per cent of all the people you meet. If they don't like you, well then be friendly and professional and think to yourself 'they must be from the other 50 per cent.'

Don't try too hard to make a good impression, but tell everyone around you that they are making a good impression.

50

HELP OTHERS TO LIKE THEMSELVES BETTER. BOOST THEIR SELF-ESTEEM

Every human being is special. The drive of every individual is to defend what lies at their inner core—call it dignity, personality, uniqueness, or even ego—against all enemies.

Remember: We are more interested in ourselves than in anything else. Everybody you will ever meet—no matter what they say—wants to feel important and become somebody of importance. Everybody in one way or another seeks the approval of their peers.

Only the ones who have learned to like themselves can be generous and friendly to others. Only if you are on good terms with yourself can you be on good terms with others. Once you start to like yourself better, only then can you begin to like others better. Only if you become more and more satisfied with yourself, can you become less critical and more tolerant toward others.

Self-acceptance and self-approval are the roots of good human relations. People with a high level of self-esteem are easy to get along with. They are balanced, happy, tolerant and willing to accept other people's ideas. Because they have taken care of themselves, they are able to take other people's needs into account. They are strong people that have no problem in admitting mistakes.

Low self-esteem people, on the other hand, are insecure, arrogant, and mistrusting. Everybody seems to be a threat to them. Behind the loud person, the show-off, the bully, the person that walks into the room like a peacock, many times there is an insecure, low self-esteem person.

If you meet this kind of person, be nice. Yes, you read right. Be nice. The rudest people sometimes need understanding the most. Arrogant behaviour is many times a cry for help, 'Hello. I want to feel important. Please notice me.' Many times these people need to beat people down so that they can increase their feeling of importance. On the other hand, they are afraid that you can see right through them, so they attack first. Be nice. Give them real compliments and genuine praise, and most of the times you will see a marvellous transformation. Look for their strengths, their good points. Things you can sincerely praise. You can get along easier with anyone if you feed their ego.

Make it a habit to see the good in people, to give them sincere compliments and watch how much better your relations with others become. Help them like themselves but better.

51

MAKE IT LOOK EASY

How many things you didn't do something because it seemed too difficult or because somebody told you that you are not good enough? We meet our limitations daily. I'm not good enough for this, I'm not good enough for that, not talented for this, too clumsy for that. When this happens, we either don't try it at all, or we give up after a short time. We think that Michael Jordan has been born a genius on the basketball court and nobody tells us that he worked countless hours on the courts, we think Michael Phelps has been born a 23 times gold medalist at the Olympics and nobody tells us he even trained 12 hours on weekends because he figured like this he will train 624 hours more per year than his competitors. We forgot that practice and repetition achieve mastery and that work and consistency beats talent every time.

When we want to learn something new we need to be reminded of these facts. We need teachers and leaders that have patience and make things look easy.

If you tell your kids, your spouse or your employees that they are too stupid to do a certain thing, not talented enough, that they're doing it all wrong, then you have killed all their aspirations right there in the beginning—if they are unfortunate enough to believe you. On the other hand, if you use encouragement, make it seem easy, tell them that nobody is born a master at his craft and that with patience and consistency they can hone their skill, then the outcome will look quite different.

Give the people around you confidence and inspire them with your belief and faith in them and see miracles happen. It's the Pygmalion Effect all over again.

Make it look easy and see people thrive.

52

USE POSITIVE TALK

Science has now found out that the way we talk about ourselves or events has a profound impact on our mindset and even our reality. People who tend to talk pessimistically in the morning tend to experience their day as much worse, while people who speak positively at the start of the day tend to experience their day as much more positive, meeting with much more opportunities. It's not rocket science. We've all experienced it.

Let's face it. It's much more fun to be around people who have a positive outlook than people who are pessimistic and are continually whining about their personal problems. Of course, we have to have an open ear to the problems of our friends and colleagues. I'm talking about those people who continuously use us as their human trash can. Unfortunately, emotions and words are also contagious, and if we spend too much time with these kind of people, they might drag us down into their dark world.

If you have problems, talk to a counselor, pastor or trusted friend. Don't go public. Describing your sufferings in public doesn't make you an attractive person, in contrary; it makes you quite boring and unattractive. Think of your friends who are publicly whining on social media. Do you find that attractive or pitiful?

If you are still tempted to air your troubles publicly, anyways do have Lou Holtz' words in mind: 'Never tell your problems to anyone…20 per cent don't care, and the other 80 per cent are glad you have them.'

And while we are at it, also eliminate teasing and sarcasm from your conversation. Above all, in public. These are not cute ways of showing affection or how smart you are. While you might hope that others will recognize your cleverness and see your fine sense of humour, to people that don't know you, you might come across as utterly offensive and lose all the chances ever to win their sympathy.

And there is another reason: Tampering with other people's self-esteem—and that's what you are doing by being sarcastic or teasing—can do a lot of damage to the person even when done in fun. You might get away with it, but there is a great risk that you will lose people and come across as rude.

So cut the crap. Eliminate complaining, sarcasm and teasing from your conversations and use positive talk.

53

BE FRIENDLY

The best way to get something from people is by being friendly. This is so basic I shouldn't even have to write about it, but I can see every day that people just seem to have 'forgotten' it. It seems that many of us live as if we were alone in the world. If you are angry or rude and just 'unload' your resentment this might be good for you, but for the other person? Will their experience make it easier for them to agree with you or to help you? I don't think so.

If you need something from someone the best way to get it is to remain friendly—even if it's difficult sometimes. Friendliness usually causes friendliness in return. Showing your anger in most cases will not get you what you want.

Being kind and friendly will make people change their minds or help you more often than being angry and start shouting matches. Try it. It works.

Dr Joseph Murphy in one of his books recommends: 'Become friendlier, the ruder they get and you will win them over.' When you have many clients a day, you have many opportunities to practice and shall I say… It works! As a waiter, I had a direct measure. The amount of my tip. When really rude people came in I saw it as a challenge to 'win them over,' and in 99 per cent of the cases, I did. This was great, and often it came accompanied by a nice tip.

It's so easy. Be friendly and reap the rewards.

54

WRITE A THANK YOU NOTE

One true magical trick when it comes to improving your relationships is writing thank you notes. Surprisingly, this is not only beneficial for the receiver but as science found out also for the sender.

If you want to take it a step further, write not only notes but entire thank you letters. While Thank you notes are a sign of politeness, kindness and valuing the receiver and boost your own well-being, thank you letters have even more impact. Studies show that gratitude letters can increase happiness and decrease depression for the person that writes it for as long as three months after the writing of the letter. It's said that the benefits are highest if you deliver the message in person. Try this even if it's just a simple e-mail to someone.

Ideally, write the email to one person who has made a major positive difference in your life and whom you have never thanked for the positive influence they had in your life. Take your time to write the note. And while you are at it…why not write to one person a week?

Gratitude is one of the single best ingredients for happiness and great relationships and the antidote to all those negative emotions which damage our relations like greed, envy, jealousy, rage, arrogance and so on. Did you notice that you can't be grateful and unhappy at the same time? You also can't be worried and grateful at the same time. And you can't be angry and grateful at the same time. Choose gratitude.

Make showing gratitude to someone every day a habit. A colleague, the cashier at the supermarket, your parents, the mailman, your kids or the basketball coach. Be creative.

It's important to feel the gratitude and really think about the things you are thanking the person for. If it's trivial or not heartfelt, it doesn't work.

Remember we are all hungry for genuine appreciation. Show other people that they matter in your life and in the world.

Show people that they are making the world a better place and write them a thank you note or a thank you email.

Part VII

....

Last But Not Least

55

BEWARE OF PEOPLE WITH FALSE SELF-ESTEEM

If you want to become attractive to people and be an influencer you have to develop real and stable self-esteem, which is not to be confused with the attitude and behaviour of people who are narcissistic, arrogant and selfish. Stay away from these people. They are displaying pseudo-self-esteem or false self-esteem and clearly demonstrate a lack of real self-esteem. False self-esteem is only the pretense of self-belief and self-respect without the reality of it. It hides behind the illusion of having the characteristics of true self-esteem, nothing else.

Someone who walks into a room showing off, bragging, looking like a peacock, probably doesn't have high self-esteem. In fact, this behaviour is the exact opposite of healthy self-esteem. If we can choose, we really don't want to be around this kind of people. To worsen matters, people with false self-esteem will always judge and value you—and themselves—by what you achieve and by your results, not for what you really are.

Stick around people with higher levels of self-esteem. Mostly, they are humble and don't need to show off continually.

Work on becoming an example. Work on your self-esteem

and display real self-esteem which is founded in reality—in actual performance, in actual success, and in actual practices. It is the product of effort and hard work.

When you show real self-esteem, you will attract people, and maybe your example will show people with false self-esteem that there is no need to protect themselves. That they can also build real self-esteem, that being wrong and vulnerable is no problem at all, but actually a sign of strength and that they can let go of arrogance, selfishness and their false sense of security.

Become a high self-esteem person and stay away from low self-esteem people except if, you can be a role model for them.

56

PUT YOURSELF IN
OTHER PEOPLE'S SHOES

Empathy is one of the keys to success in our relationships with other people. It's easy to judge and condemn people, any fool can do that. It's a lot harder to try to understand them. If you have the patience, make an effort to understand them, to find out what makes them tick and you can achieve anything and surely people will love to be around you.

Put yourself in other person's shoes. Why do they do what they do? What's the underlying reason? How would you react and feel in the same situation? This is the key to all human relations. Your success in dealing with other people depends on to what extent you are able to understand them, to put yourself in their shoes, to see things from their point of view.

When you start considering other people's feelings, ideas and standpoints to be as important as your own the reactions will be very positive. Tell people what YOU would like to hear and encourage them to share their feelings and insights.

Communicate with empathy. Seeing things from other person's standpoint will avoid arguments and tensions before they start. Before asking anyone to buy your product or giving orders just stop a minute and ask yourself, 'Why would my client/employee/spouse will want to do this?'

Practice putting yourself in the other person's shoes. You will have far fewer arguments and disagreements and far better results.

Always think regarding the other person's point of view.

57

BE SYMPATHETIC WITH
THE OTHER PERSON

'I don't blame you. If I were you, I would surely feel just as you do.' Add this phrase to your vocabulary. It will stop arguments; it will eliminate ill feelings, it will create goodwill and surely make the other person listen more closely to you.

We have said it before. Don't judge people. Everyone you meet is fighting their own battle, and we don't know anything about it. If people are rude, irritated, mad, don't judge them for being as they are and instead feel sorry for them. Pity them. The only thing they probably want is somebody to care for their battle, some sympathy. Be that someone.

When someone attacks, you apologize and sympathize with their point of view. This will make them apologize and sympathize with your point of view. If you manage the art of answering to an insult with kindness and sympathy, the world is yours.

It's nearly magical. Sympathy and kindness neutralize rudeness, anger, contempt and all the other hard feelings.

If you want something, you won't get anywhere with threats

and a loud voice. Use sympathy instead. Ask kindly, and doors will open, and things will get done.

We all crave for sympathy. If you want to win people over start practicing.

58

DON'T MAKE ASSUMPTIONS

One of the most significant sources of trouble in all human relationships is misunderstandings, and one huge reason for misunderstandings is that we constantly make suppositions. We suppose what other people think or believe, and the worst is we take our assumptions for real and react to them, and from there it's drama all the way. The problem is that most of the time, what we suppose is not even true. It's made up in your mind. Assumptions destroy friendships, marriages, relationships at work—and all of this because we forget to do one thing: ASK.

It's always better to ask than to make assumptions, but of course, asking takes courage, and it's a lot more comfortable to make assumptions, but if we have the big picture in our mind we notice that asking creates clarity while assumptions create suffering.

In our romantic relationships, we suppose that our partner can read our mind and get mad if they can't guess what we want and don't meet our expectations. 'You should have known.' 'How could you not have known' yadda yadda yadda. Come on!

If somebody doesn't call us, we make assumptions, and if they do, we also do. If we don't understand something, we suppose what it means instead of asking what it really means.

We suppose that others see life the same way we do, we suppose that they think and feel like we do, we even make assumptions about ourselves, about what we can and cannot do—the latter most of the time without even checking if we could actually do it if we had put in the time to learn it (or watch a YouTube video on how to do it).

So, once and for all, the best way to get rid of all those limiting and hurting assumptions is to ASK. Get clarity. Confirm that you really understand what they are telling you. Don't be afraid. Once you know the answer, you don't need to make assumptions anymore. The truth will be laid out right in front of you and you can use your energy for more important things.

When you stop making assumptions, and start to ask questions, your communication will reach a new level of clarity, free from mind-movies, imagined worst-case scenarios and judgment. Even better: once your communication is clear, all your relationships will change dramatically—some for the better, some for the worse (let the latter ones go).

Stop making assumptions and start asking questions. It will change everything.

59

DON'T TAKE ANYTHING
PERSONALLY

This is a tough one to write for me. I struggled a long time with taking everything personally and I still do every now and then. Do yourself one favour and don't take anything that happens around you personally. Even if somebody calls you an idiot. It's not you; it's them. Really. Most of the time it has nothing to do with you. It's the projection of their own problems onto you (except if everybody you meet calls you an idiot, in that case, do some thinking and self-reflection).

If you take everything personally, you will suffer a lot and be an easy victim for manipulators and people who want to hurt you (yup! They are out there…). You'll get offended easily and will be defensive all the time.

Whatever people say to you—the good or the bad—is none of your business. Only YOU have to know who you are. Get over the need to be right. Remember what you want: To be right or to be in peace? Be smart. Choose peace.

I mentioned before that what hurts you is not what other people say to you, it's what you say to yourself afterward. It's the wounds that are still not healed within you. If you know that you are not an idiot; me saying you are an idiot will not affect you. Same as it doesn't affect you if I say you have blue hair when you clearly don't.

When I take things personally and get hurt, I pause and reflect, 'Why is this affecting me?', 'Do I deep inside myself maybe think that what I'm reacting to is true?'

You can only be affected by somebody calling you an idiot, a bad writer, a bad spouse, if somewhere deep inside you, you think you are.

So whatever people say, think or do—don't take it personally. Don't even make your own opinion about yourself too personal. And always remember what Dr Wayne Dyer once said, 'How people treat you is their Karma, how you react to it is yours.'

Save yourself some suffering and don't take anything personally.

60

STOP SPENDING TIME WITH THE WRONG PEOPLE

We are talking a lot about getting along with people, being friendly, showing empathy in this book, but sometimes the best techniques are just not good enough. As I said in the beginning, this book is not about becoming a people-pleaser. It's about honest, good relationships. The truth is you can't get along well with everybody you meet and sometimes it just doesn't click. You might be trying to apply what you learned in this book and still just don't get through to people. Wayne Dyer once said to accept that 50 per cent of the people you meet in your life won't like you, no matter what you do, no matter how nice you are, no matter how good you are. So, if you meet somebody that just doesn't like you, think to yourself, 'Well, I guess this is just one from the other 50 per cent' and move on. And even more important: don't try to change yourself so that they like you or spend time with you. It's useless. Stay authentic.

Sometimes, you even have to answer to rude, arrogant and bullying type of people right back in the way they come on to you. Trying to get along with people doesn't mean that you can't set boundaries or that you have to let people walk all over you. It's totally okay and even necessary to set boundaries that others can't overstep.

If you want to improve anything in life, your self-esteem, success, happiness you need to watch very, very closely who you spend your time with. Stay away from the toxic people and instead choose the positivity of people that support your life. Choose to be around people who help you with your strengths, stay away from people who belittle you and by God…let go of relationships that constantly hurt you.

Spend your time with people that help you to motivate yourself, gain courage, and help you take the right actions. Stay away from those who drain your energy, disrespect you and drag you down. If you are around them for too long, they can convert you into a negative and cynical person over time.

Jim Rohn once said that you are the average of the five persons you spend the most time with and science has proven it over and over again since then. Attitudes and emotions are highly contagious. So, once again. Spend your time with people who motivate you, believe in you, and bring out the best in you. Be around people who empower you.

Life is too short to spend time with people who don't treat you with love and respect. Let them go and make new friends.

61

GET RID OF PERFECTIONISM

If you are the type of person that needs other people to be perfect in relationships, you are doomed to encounter unhappiness in your relationships because nobody can ever live up to your high standards. Perfectionism is the enemy of good relations, because very often perfectionists are extremely sensitive to criticism, and always on the defensive. It gets even worse when we expect perfectionism from our spouse, partners, or friends. If you expect other people to be perfect, you will inevitably get disappointed which leads to frustrations and in the worst case to lack of acceptance of the spouse, friend or partner.

Perfectionism also harms our relationships indirectly, because it hurts our self-esteem and our lack of self-esteem then hurts our relationships. The constant feeling of failure and the lack of self-acceptance that many perfectionists experience drains their self-esteem and at the same time make it impossible to develop healthy self-esteem.

Perfectionists are also less likely to try, and less likely to put themselves on the line, which are two of the main ingredients to happiness and healthy relationships. They also experience a lot of anxiety and stress in their relationships because there is a constant fear of failure.

Instead of being a perfectionist in your relationships, become a person committed to excellence. Accept that perfection does not exist. It's enough to always give your best. Sometimes it gets you close to perfect, many times it doesn't. No problem. If you can really own this truth—you might have to practice a lot—you will experience far less anxiety and frustration and far better relationships.

You will go from only experiencing—at best—a temporary relief to enjoying the journey of your life, with its ups and downs and imperfections, and much higher levels of happiness in life in general and in your relationships. Try it! It works.

Get rid of perfectionism and enjoy lasting satisfaction in your relationships.

62

SOLVE YOUR PROBLEMS
RIGHT AWAY

Did you ever notice that some people spend more time and energy avoiding and dancing around their problems, blaming others for them, than in trying to solve them?

Did you notice that it's not a lot of fun to be around people who always have problems—and even worse—just talk about those and don't make the slightest attempt to solve them?

Well, I have something better for you.

To make sure you don't become one of these people; solve your problems right away. Face them right now. Start working on solutions, NOW. Dancing around them or running away from them makes no sense because they will come after you. They will pursue you. If you don't solve them, they will repeat themselves over and over again until you learn something and are ready to move on. Or even worse: If you don't solve them, they will become even bigger and one day blow up right in your face. If we don't solve our problems life usually finds its way, and it's usually worse than dealing with it in the first place. Think accident, illness, lawsuit, etc.

Did you ever notice that you may continue to encounter

the same set of problems until you stop and solve the recurring problems? For example, in multiple romantic relationships.

Not taking responsibility or trying to postpone your problems is just a giant waste of energy. The only thing it does is increase your level of anxiety and give you sleepless nights, feeling really bad.

Believe me, once you go against all your (imagined?) fears and confront and solve the problem, you'll feel much better and find out that it was a lot less painful to face the problem and solve it, than the whole process of dancing around it.

If you see your problems as 'challenges,' 'learning opportunities,' 'opportunities for growth,' or even 'blessings' it might be even easier for you to deal with them and solve them right away.

Life is facing one problem after another. The difference is how you face those problems, how you deal with them and what you learn from them. Looking back at the problems you had in your life—didn't each one of them have something positive? Maybe a loss in business saved you from an even more significant loss because you learned from it. In real hard times, it can be very beneficial for you to adopt the belief that life/God/the universe only puts a problem in your way if you are able to solve it!

Solve your problems right away and enjoy much better relationships.

CONCLUSION

Dear friend. You have come to the end of this little book! It has been a true pleasure to make the beginning of your journey together with you—yet this is only the beginning.

I sincerely hope you had as much fun reading this little book as I had writing it. But by now you know: reading it is not enough to take your relationships to the next level. The knowledge of these little tricks and techniques alone won't serve you to improve your relationships with people and influence them. It's the application of this knowledge that will take your personal and professional relationships to the next level. You have many valuable tools in your toolbox now. It's up to you to use them.

If you want a better life, more happiness, more success and better relationships with friends, colleagues, partners, and family start applying this knowledge from TODAY onwards. Put it into practice in your everyday life.

You don't have to do everything at once. Start small. Choose the proposals you like best and start practicing them in your daily life. By now, you know that some small changes can build up to something huge over time—just like compound interest. These are proven and time-tested methods. They work. The problem is that generally, only a small percentage of people apply them. Become part of this group. Become a doer—it will be worth it.

Your attitude will be crucial. Keep a positive mindset even when things don't go that well. Remember, sometimes when we are working towards a goal we get tested. When I was writing this book about how to influence people and have significant relationships, I got into more 'strange' situations with people than ever before. I'm convinced these were tests so that I can apply the learned characteristics right away.

The same might happen to you. Be prepared to apply what you have learned.

If you have any feedback or questions, don't hesitate to get in touch with me. My email is marc@marcreklau.com. I answer every email, so please do drop me a line if there's anything you'd like to ask or if you have any suggestions for improvement.

I wish you all the success in the world with people. Go and take your life to the next level.

All the best.

Marc

ONE LAST THING...

If you have been inspired by my books and want to help others to reach their goals and improve their lives, here are some action steps you can take immediately to make a positive difference:

Gift my books to friends, family, colleagues and even strangers so that they can also learn that they can reach their goals and live great lives.

Please share your thoughts about this book on Twitter, Facebook and Instagram or write a book review. It helps other people to find my books.

If you own a business or if you are a manager—or even if you're not—gift some copies to your team or employees and improve the productivity of your company.

Contact me at marc@marcreklau.com.